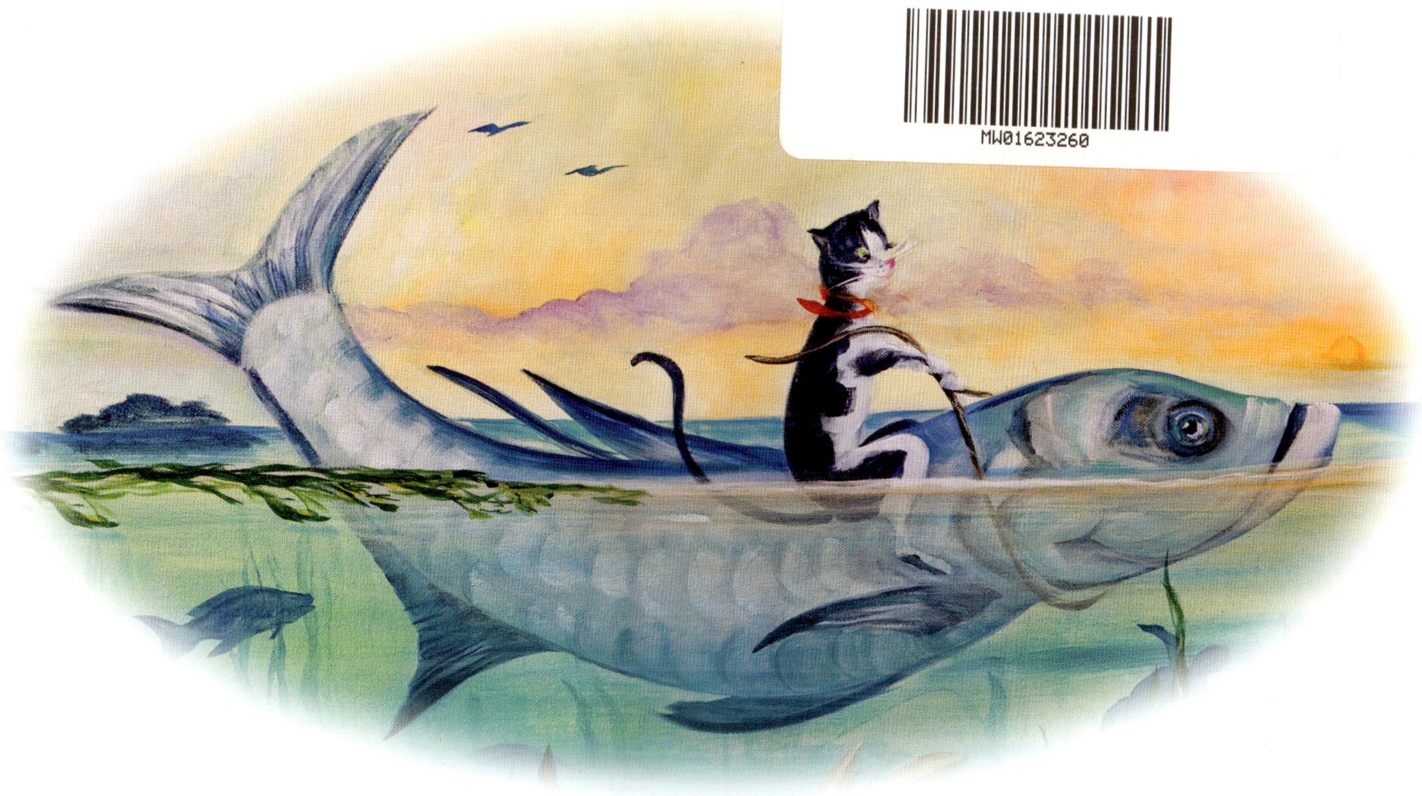

COSMO THE BOAT CAT

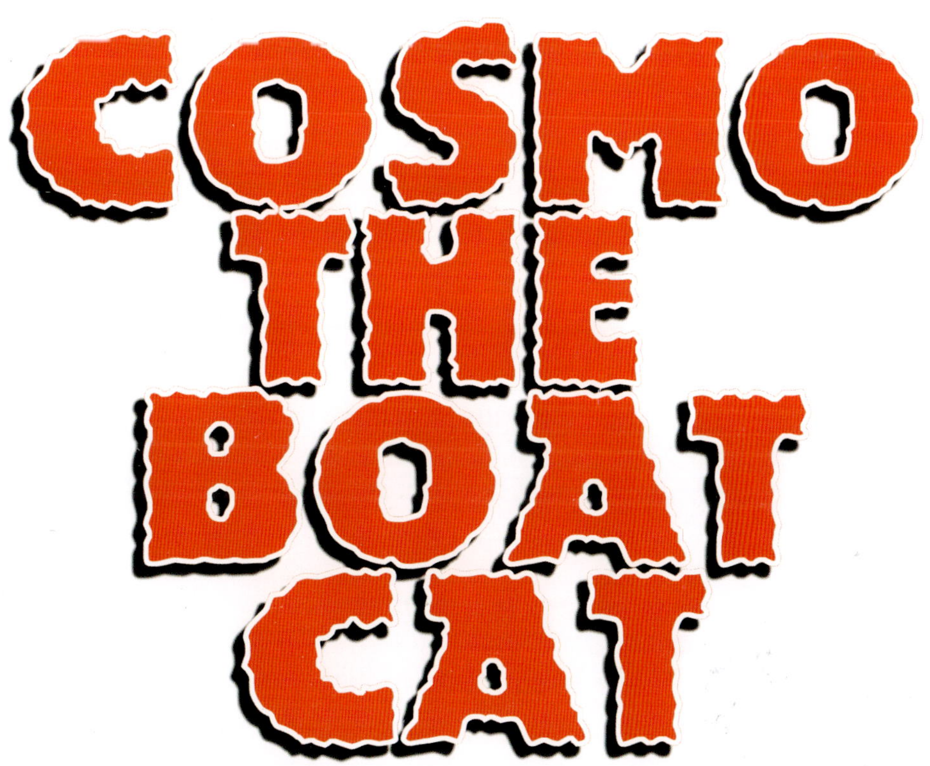

Created and Illustrated by Sherry Sweet Tewell

Co-Written by Marky Pierson

Edited by Carol Tedesco

Title *Cosmo the Boat Cat*

Published by Sweet T Publishing, Key West, Florida

Library of Congress Control Number: 2009906270
ISBN: 9780615303666

Sweet T Publishing
P.O. Box 4025
Key West, Florida 33041

www.sherrytewell.com
artbabe00@aol.com

To my children, Lindsey and Zach, who told the best stories.
Thank you Zach for bringing home the pick of the litter.
MOM

To Chad my Hero.
SST

Cosmo the Cat always wore a tuxedo with a red tie;
He lived happily in a house and he never asked WHY
Or WHAT was beyond his big front door;
Sleeping all day long he never wanted for more.
But over the fence and beyond the trees,
Cosmo would soon find out about the big blue sea.

Fish

Fish
Tale

Change was coming for Cosmo, an amazing change of scene,
A dazzling new home he could not picture in a dream.
Melody announced as she burst through the door,
"We are going to make a change Cosmo – We're doing it for sure!
Off to the ocean, above the fishes we will float,
We're off to the sea Cosmo! We'll live on a *houseboat*!"

Cosmo whimpered just a little then started to cry,
“Cats don’t like water he yelped,” with a sniffle and a sigh.
Melody scooped him up and dried his cat tears,
“Outside of these doors there is nothing to fear.
I know you’re not sure Cosmo, I can see it on your face,
But living on the ocean is like no other place!”

Cosmo finally grabbed a few things to take;
He walked down the dock, with every step his legs did shake.
But a gentle and deep voice came from below,
Marvin the Manatee surfaced and welcomed Cosmo,
"Hello my little fellow!"

Marvin came every morning and said “Hello” and “Goodbye;”
Seagulls hovered over the boat squawking “Hola” and “Hi.”
But Harvey the Heron always seemed too busy,
He danced along the boat rails making Cosmo dizzy.
Cosmo wanted to know all about Harvey’s WHO and WHY,
But Harvey never answered and he just scooted on by.

One fateful morning when Cosmo was asleep,
Harvey landed on his head, bounced and leaped.
Cosmo spun around and his legs started to slip,
"I'm sliding into the water Harvey! I'm going to take a dip!"
Cosmo reached out for Harvey – holding on with all of his might,
As Cosmo splashed into the water, Harvey flew out of sight!

Cosmo closed his eyes tight as he fell from the boat,
He started to cat-paddle but was not able to float.
He started to sink – he did not like that at all,
Then he felt something hard under his little cat paw.
A deep voice from below bellowed out with a laugh,
"My name is Thelonious and I will be your life raft!"

Cosmo opened his eyes and he let out a sigh,
Thelonious chuckled, "Hold on little guy!
I'm a wise old turtle," he said with a wink.
"Would you like to come on an adventure? What do you think?
There are many friends to meet out in the deep blue,
Manatees, Eagle Rays and Mermaids – how does that sound to you?"

Cosmo straightened himself up and held on tight,
With a flipper swoosh they were out of sight.
When just in the shallows – a ways off from the beach,
A large shiny fish came almost within reach.
"Hey Cosmo, this is Louie the Tarpon – he is real big and strong,"
Louie smiled just a little and then Cosmo jumped on!

They went through the mangroves and headed out deep,
When Cosmo was startled by a splash and a leap.
Louie explained that dolphins jump really high,
Just as a dorsal fin reached for the sky!
It was Dusty the Dolphin – with her newborn calf;
They all danced and played and had a good laugh.

Dusty waved goodbye and raced out of sight,
They dove to the coral reef much to Cosmo's delight.
Thelonious swooped over to visit another old friend,
Charles was an Eagle Ray – he shimmered with every bend.
Cosmo was amazed by this colorful place,
Such beautiful new friends put a large smile on his face.

"Cosmo, this is Charles he sings all day long."
"Check this out Cosmo – I'm going to sing you a song."
Cosmo wanted to jump off Thelonious
and dance upon the reef . . .

But Charles sang slowly as Cosmo listened with disbelief,

The Reef will die if you touch it
and on the Reef we all rely,
So you can only look Cosmo
and always remember why!

They swam deeper and Cosmo could not believe his ears,
The sounds and the glow brought Cosmo to tears.
Harmony the Mermaid was singing a beautiful song;
She waved them over and asked them to sing along.
Everything was magical, it was like a dream,
Dancing in the deep blue sea – a fantastical scene.

Some fish danced this way – the seaweed swayed like that,
Cosmo flew through the water – a happy little cat.
Confident and strong in his underwater space,
Cosmo feels lucky to have seen such an amazing place.
"The world is much bigger than I ever thought before,
There must be more friends to meet – I must see more!"

REEF RELIEF is a global nonprofit membership organization dedicated to preserving and protecting living coral reef ecosystems. Coral reef are delicately-balanced underwater environments, home to fish, hard and soft corals, sponges, jellyfish, snails, crabs, lobsters, rays, sea turtles and other sea life. They are the oldest ecosystem on earth, yet they cover less than 1% of the total ocean. Corals have existed for over 400 million years and reached their current level of diversity 50 million years ago. Reef Relief relies on memberships, contributions and volunteer efforts. Join our grassroots efforts to save coral reefs. www.reefrelief.org.

Save the Manatee Club was established in 1981 by singer / songwriter Jimmy Buffett and former U.S. Senator and Florida Governor, Bob Graham, to protect manatees and their aquatic habitat for future generations. Today, it is the world's leading manatee conservation organization. The Club is a membership-based, national nonprofit organization that promotes public awareness and education; sponsors regional and international scientific research and rescue, rehabilitation, and release efforts; advocates for the conservation of manatees and their essential habitat; and takes legal action when necessary. To learn more about manatees visit www.savethemanatee.org

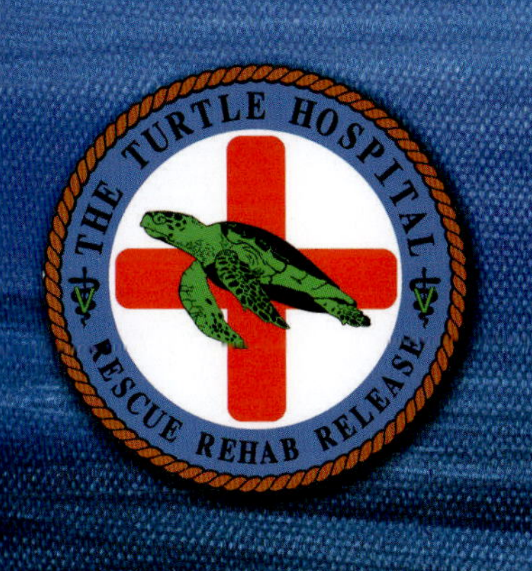

The Turtle Hospital in Marathon, FL, is the only certified veterinary clinic in the world specifically for sea turtles. Since 1986, over 1000 sick and injured sea turtles have been rescued, rehabilitated, and released back to the ocean. In addition to rescuing sea turtles, the Turtle Hospital also conducts public education programs, assists with research in conjunction with state universities, and works for environmental legislation to make the beaches and waters safe and clean for turtles. To learn more about the Turtle Hospital and current patients please visit www.turtlehospital.org.

Cosmopolitan Von Moxie Sweet Tewell